AUX/ARC
TRYPT ICH

AUX/ARC TRYPT ICH

Poppycock & Assphodel; Winter;
A Night of Dark Trees

CODY-ROSE CLEVIDENCE

NIGHTBOAT BOOKS
NEW YORK

ISBN: 978-1-64362-112-8

Cover art: Cody-Rose Clevidence
Design and typesetting by Rissa Hochberger
Typeset in Garamond 3 and Cardinal Photo

Cataloging-in-publication data is available from
the Library of Congress

ACKNOWLEDGEMENTS

My endless thanks to the journals where some of these poems first appeared: *Dusie,
Touch the Donkey, Horseless Review, Bomb Cyclone, Baest, Hold: a Journal, Slow Poetry in
America Newsletter, Aurochs, Yalobusha Review*, and to Garden Door Press for putting
out *Poppycock & Assphodel* as a very pretty chapbook.

Nightboat Books
New York
www.nightboat.org

CONTENTS

WINTER
61

A NIGHT OF DARK TREES

"an ordinary error placed me here"

in the serotonin corridors of my wilderness   in the neural
nets are caught   in the mackerellight & ozone of my heart
in the tense muscle of a crocus   olfactory bulb of my acre
prime sublingual rib   lost in the magnum
opus of my heart   independent   of   void   most
utterly devoid of song   tiny hummingbird   of my eyes violet
quarrel deep in the forests verbage   of my heart redundant
of crocus   redundant of dogwood & redbud   as petals
fall triumphant   so too   I am at a loss   & will blind
the cathedrals of my knowing   with the overabundant scripture
of my heart   will salivate copiously & with abandon
in the blue gloaming   I mean groaning   of my heart
in the citadel   the sap salty in the flexed limbs   the mist dripping
off each leaf   called to each   I call to each I say
"leaf" I say "violet" I say "mist" I say "dogtooth violet"   I say
"how can I possibly bear whatever grief will inevitably come towards
me through all the corridors of my life"   I say "I will blind the
cathedrals of my knowing" I say "I will douse the careless peony"
"I will vie earnestly & with moderate valor" "I will curse fervently &
gesticulate also"   "I will have numerous & varied loves"
"I will try to not drink so much"   "I will strain the verb of my
being into the dim groaning"   "as too I strain my sight there"
"I succumb henceforth & wholeheartedly" "eventually I will get up
from wherever I have laid myself down"   the falcons too must eat
in the endless neurobiology   of the forest
the delicate, the careless   lichen   of my eyes
I swallow the great creek of dusk in me   it calls up a surge in me
it goes along into the dark   it goes along into the dark

Poppycock
& Assphodel

for everything to come

"I am fond of hunting" he said, "I know th
woods, but I have never seen such a shaft"
—PHOCUS, OF SOME BRO'S JAVELIN, OVID

[I think there is
a beast er ix in my
sodden ryth
mic hum
drum thun
der bolt
ed throat]

.

.

.

.

[song u x say
say sea
son say see
cret crea
ture turn
sweet
ly the
creek
in me
at all
ways
rush
in me
b lush
in me
over]
x]

.

.

[so sleep in my
dark bummer of
castrated
stars]

.

[*m*ooring
-ourning
oaring
,sore
]   or,

      "gloriole"]

      lol

//

]

[u r x ult ed in yr

buttercup palm be

grateful]

[goddamnit

[
night o might
might muse be
beckon come
back jagg
ed whip
or will ow
allow all
low oh
O ow
I etch,
I, loon.]
∴

[mortified, I]

[moon u]

       [this is a most
       heinous aperture
       in my cockscomb
       by the sea]

]

[o eye
ram u
idle i's

for
lorn

for
loin

tender *of*]

                          [lion eyed lunatic
    /   moth
                          aplomb buttock
                          moron, flute]

[with what acute eye]

I,I,I,

    [rim the butthole of the sun]

[this
ven
trical
twi
light
this
mon
ster
ous
dead
pan
blue
scalp
el
day
burnt
to
a
crisp!]

[
marsh blue
bell you
does this
hurt
yes

r u sure?

yes

]

//
trust
me

]

no
way

dude.

.

[

[
dirge goes great with butter
                    lover
                    plunder

hymn goes good with

             poppycock & assphodel

]

//

[

gloat, mote
dumb, rhyme
petite, mort
pterodactyl

blue, pfhhh
geyser, spy
arkedelphia
lazy, eye

14

unshamed, sun
thoughts, sensations
goat, boat
sudden, come

perilous, eagle-eye
perpendicular, lizard-sky
lamb-of-god, whippoorwill
masochist, [thy] animal

all-the-way, magnificent
cluster-fuck, accident—
dodecahedron, demi-god
parallax, "kiss thy rod"

vertebrate, cortisol
mandrake, parasol
mighty storm, entourage
take me down, little dove,

milky way, vital ounce
oxytocin, palindrome
this glee is mine
it's "born within"

]

[

    srysly,
    wtf
    [?]

[

"paradoxical, paradisical fruit
issue forth, there"

is it weeping
no

it's more like
[   ]
the opposite

    but
    sometimes
    it's
    like
    weeping,
    sure.

]

[

moon I eye] am marble of & suffer
its roundness in me now] & [4ever]

.

.

In the soft
light of day

I ask u

in yr hand
some

my thorn
some

shock
dew

or
do not

I don't
care

any
way

dome of flinch— & catch & leaf & pry
leaf off, &— switch— no thrust joist just
bract, brace or limb, held, hymn down,
hymnal, throat, succumb— all full up
w succumbing, come *on*
it's *becoming*:

haggard in the gasping
buzzard of glimpse
sparrows foot

fuck u
// angel

yr no angel

let up

don't.

]

["miracle" "of the rose" uranus—lol—
I'll trade this rhyme-scheme for a rose [u wld]
a trilling leap upon it & a curse—

sideways is— the glory
& hazy is— the light—

git 'er done— in moss-light []
callousd n polished of strum

surround [x] w an "asphodel"
a clover and a word

surround [x] w paradigm
a timid breath a fist of grass
a dozer & a world—

]

[root in swoon
swoon in rut
swan en route
swan in gut,
a flute.

]

Petunia, petulance, numbskull, pestilence,
foxglove (poisonous) morning-star,
happenstance, ring-cycle, little dove, hard
winter, _____ [love]

Slip-shod, daisy chain, oxymoron, lions-mane,
curse of knowing, eyelid noise, sucker punch,
to-dull-the-pain—

to dwell there, mitigate, fovea, aspirate,
solemnly, dormant seed, rend asunder,
— hesitate—

[[

Hercules,
Scruff of Mtns,

grind her—

.

]

[tickle / me
// pink izzit
mtns rise //
so sun // so]

.

[x squelch & suckle//
x cripple & hive]

.

[x 4x4xplorer
x 4x4xplored
I x I imp
lore x
x I xp lore /
    I   ode]

.

---

jewelweed seedpod : google it

deleted jargon of sadness — [] th' glitter / of it [breaks]
what my eyes | purge them | what my eyes
{purge them} lilaceous — I mean purple, but |
   [fuck baptism, but]
be doused {come sudden} th' spring I reckon [comes]
verily | morphic | be | {ye dim of blink or shook }
rhyme crash on leaf as leaf crash on leaf | {wut}

uncastrated
]in the citadel

soggy petunia dude iris oh | excess in th eagle
of my noun | joy in th' chokehold of my verb | relentless
in the citadel {"of becoming"} [wut?] : ["I"] ride "the lightning" ;
| (the hive, relentless—)
  ["I"] swarm & buckle ; ["I"] whimper only— |

s[welt]er a rose, or whip]p]oor{will} or tilt or
bend {over} | or {bend} back | speak this gibberish {o} {lol}
I rile my eyes I preen them o I toss them about; reckless in th' .
half-light in th' pink-light in th' sound [] the reverb's reverb

like a garden. like a cup
of garden, there—

& gather up, & scatter—
& gather up, & scatter—

] "I" reckon it mightily—
] "I" drench | mine "eyes"

]

{...}

[

the gems r in/ the forest therr/ & by thy look
be kept/ & gouge thy eyes that sparkle there
& go & gouge/ & be among the hidden things
& be a rock/ grows soft the moss/ therr.   ]

.

[

sycamore [] dendrite of the
wint/er woods

violet behind   the
tangle—this—

eyes gorged   [] on violet
racket of thr Ozark [] immaculate
orc/estra xempt [] a shadow
doubtless [] lashes
me [] a shadow
down [] deep
dim [] dumb
in [] me

bell

blue as th see
dumb as th see

]

[

in the wild [] lavender light
[my] eyes r full [] to the brim / w. it

]

[
x say re
gret go loom
-inous in
us
go boom go blue
-ming in us go
& gouge or gorge
yr gorgeous
eye what
can
survive

what
ever

this

]

[

izzat a geode
no

it's just an ordinary ~~ode~~
                    ~~god~~
                    rock

         [is it it is
         is it] crush
         ing] it is—

..
.

.

this then there is the
arc is this then there my
sun is of over let it go
there it is a ringlet of
is a circlet clasp then
is the zero of the moon
ringing or is it clinging
then there was another
sunk inside the other one

]

[

please o
please
take
me
back
2
the
paradise
city
where the grass
is—

a circlet I—
lay down in.
]

[

dis/ Claim/ Dis
I claim X-
claim I
pursue
loom, I egret,
in this dis
sea
sun

am lorn
lone a
laid
claim
on this
dis
chord

chord
ate choir
come, eat

a river of— .

       something there
       is rushing, rushing

       can you catch it
       no you can't

    ]

[

land—
 tender] no
glow | u rain, shine
| gloat in rhyme
rim beckon | back
my gaze is
mine.

?

]

[

who wore it best—the rattlesnake—
dawns venom then—
who came away— with vowels wrung
from every ordinary | song—
is everything —awake?

]

[NOPE]

—I'll not
thinly consummate
unbroken maw or, tongue
soft, I'll not, hard th' fold, dew
or dew not I'll not
know, I'll unknot, untongue
unknow, unlimb th' tree, moon,
cover me, now, limb, I, limb I, unlimb, un-tie   thrush I
thrush eye
unthrust know no thirst I'll not
unknow a sing
-gle thing
I swear—

or, curse—

.

.

.

lung   unlung   ungrin   grinlung
disallow   unlung
no grape

]perdition.

.

gob
let
go

no

unroam

unallowed

]fruition

.
.
.

let—
—go
— no

unlet—

unthightwig2bark
unlip2unbark unriverup unupwell 2surface,face,face
ungroin lung ungrasp
unadmire
grinadmire

grinadmiresilent
no leaf
unthunder
.

.

chagrin
cyborg
opus
no.

unhum
ungrope

.

nope.

.

opine.

unlunge

.

unnape
unname
unurgent
uncaress
galloped
uncallous
hear

this

un-is
this

&

mock
claim, dis—

.

most
allow
dis
avowel
but
o
I un.

.

most medium
rare most ear
nose hair most
twig no serrated
unserrated unpupil

untongue that   ungrape
there

unthere
in
theory

undom
mitrial
]scape

.
un-in me
how un-in me
how-to
un
in
me
be

.

unhymn him
don't unhymn me

in mortal eye
Gomorrah, leaf.

unfall
.

imbibe. unbitter root
unroot
untaste
untongue
unglue

unglory there unsung
unheroic unsun unmulberry up
unnipple unhive unletter alphabet
unnoise those noises unnight
the night up oh no

unwent I go up
the path there
"as if for the 1st time"
then unwind even that, back

ungo
uncome

.

unnorth. ungentle. no,
too un gentle, un-ungentle

u can't un ungentle

yes u can

.

ellipse
not
unnot
notunknot
twist
not "unweary"
not not
(not unkiss thy rod)
etc—

oh, no.
un o no
un oh know
o now
disavow

]for[bidden]
]meristem
]bolt & reverb
unverb
ungrasp
ungasp

the ungrape
ther

.

unlimb unhorse   hoarse
o hoarse. not unstallion not ungrape not not unask
not not unanswer, [did the truth, —] I said
unask I said unanswer

now i
unsay
even
this

rare
prayer

unprey
apex @
last

alone ther

underwent

]unpredator
]unlimb
]jargon
]unspeak

.

unpurpled eye unpurpled net
yet   unbruise
unneck

unhair
unfist

un noun
un verb
un begin

.

re iterate

how many times iterate
how many times, allow

a vowel
a stallion
2 be

purple
zenith
beneath

]foliage
]punishment

]cathedral

it was the sun that shook
it was the thrust & the pull
of the sun that shook
that littered the ground
with this.

it was the green, the green & the blue
the green & the filtering of light,
it was the rough & the tumble of light
that shook & that trembled
that came hard forth in the light
& the dark.

it was the green that took, the eye, caught
the rimmed horizon of light, that brutal
unyielding communion, shock of the surface,
shock of the deep, it was the sun came hard
in my palm on my wrist.

yeah right

dude.

]

I demean the parade
of stars] I supine
the cedar
& firs
I masochist
the "dawn" &
the "dew" I callous
the ordinary
bloom
in daylight I show
my face 2 the face
of the sun, (in more
ways than one)
I break as the
"crest" of a "wave"
in eyelet or silence
or come, "crest
fallen" in cocks-comb
or plume, I make
a pasture climb
2 th sky
w my eye,
stroke "thigh"
or rhyme "I"
with "my"
I hereby condemn
any solemn
moment

its pollen
or spume

I harvest a meadow
of larks, laugh
w th laughter
of doves
wring drip
after drip
"just th'
tip" of a star,
ther, ask
a question
in th' form
of an answer
form of a gather
or an after
-thought, thought-
less, caught
a ruby-throated hum
from th' sword-fights
of noon, the lazy
sword-fights of summer
of haze or lovers
dazed, or odor
of vowels, sprung
forth & faster,
faster & O
timid,
timid is the
flatulence of stars.

o dude of all o daffodil
o dude of a daffodil of sprung
a bolt of reason might
hold-up (unlikely) against a trumpet, not
poised, unpoised, be milked thy milky
way of trumpets, thy milky
way of aster, thy milky eye
w its ooze on its sleaze on
its griefs of, & pollen,
get down on yr knees of,
shock of grass in th fist of
(if only) a thought could rise
like th sun, forgetting
its early plum—

th' early urge 2
rage, th' plundered
urge 2 plumb.

Dude, the terror there
is lit w laugher—dude the arching
& th' archer 2

Dude the creek is rushing,
rushing | "give me but one
firm place 2 stand"

we susurrate & eagle
-stoke crudely in rhyme
flourish, hard or
eager in th' zenith
n eager th' tumult
th' cascade a shook thing
down from, night-
fall get yr
shine on
timid, there, utter
no hard consonants
what is it th' whim
of, carapace or escapade,
coronal hum pre
tidal, vault of acre
vault of all & wolf it
down, deep, throat,
grim diadem grimey
digitalis grinning in th' verb
corrosive, in th' verb
hard limbic, in th' verb
unverbed &
reverb'd glib in th'
deep where it took

GR]APES OF TH' OPP]OSITE OF WRATH : BEND]OVERBEND]BACK

I resent th' lily its bloom, I regret th' dawn of its loom
I descend th' posture of stairs, put on airs, fight "fire"
w th calm gaze of noon— huzzah— my eyes r "ashine"
in th' "gloom" I limp w a glimpse of "astride" b outside
in th' "open" too soon, sing thus: *thee thine* or cuss
my hand at my back, th wind howls its vowels at dusk it
calls something up, it "aflutter" or "startle" or "cup"

I beacon th excess of stars
w a stare w a glare of th grace
of a face, am forlorn in th dusk, dip my tusk
in a mare, (j/k we're all
geldings here) pair
pears w th' grins
of th flesh,
press leaf upon
leaf, under-leaf, leaf-thrust,
trust no utterance, can't carry
a tune.

save but for {regale me} save {face} 2 face
driven {2 what} {what have} have I {eye}
save but for {this} what. a thicket {grows}
around. {self-conscious in the wilderness
of my consciousness} 2 day: spare yellow leaves bracket
light : bright lichen on wet bark : fog low
in the holler descending : some internet
on th' internet : low drone of a small plane
{everyonceandawhile}overhead: {someoneelses
motion elliptical arnd me}: haze of all
& I {I} {1} a cusp in me {2} a bearing down
{3} soft th' tether, harness tho {4} save {but for}
a certain {glow}—

claim only the ape in apex, the prayer
in predator, lewd form in the quintet of stars. go forth my dogs,
slouch & play my dogs, hunting moths in th dappled light—
th blackberries of my eyes, my hymnals chosen pitch. I the lips
my fingers touch, go forth untriumphant & yet get thou,
get you gallant, get thrashed, grasp'd & "had th' scent on"— this
& thus, & thistle lead {me} willingly, go. it gapes me. fuck w,
lathe me, as when it, bramble it nerve up, as when wood-
roses do shed their small petals {w just a touch} it shake them
down as when it gallivant th' light down &, parse &
leave it, there, laying there, hybrid in th' meadow
is the self I'd lay {willingly, or} claim,
laid, down u {thicket} a tangle in yr eyes—
& th' petals, well, let them {go}

this there where then the whole
sky the whole pasture clambers up

 it lit rim it supine I'll

pin down] hold
down] in
truth] with a shy
ruthlessness]   abscond (my face, is it, struck
                              a beam
                                  there) [relentless in th'

              plumage of "morn" call this "dew"
           say "ew" call out
            "it trembles" [all
        particulate [& ringing th'
-------]sun, up &] cup & down, [& crown, there.

growliest March tendril   loomy night forlorn
ploddingly down   my dove   let us   most
growliest and lorn of   let us   let me   may I
who else   and, of   here   stay   still in the
fullness of   when u r grown   a corridor in u
& when the dark   it fills the creekbed first   then
grows full   here, most owl most silent   wingbeat
may I   an owl of

let, no, go—

a mocking thing   a lock & key   eiderdown   done
duckling gone tulip-tip th' spring & then   when by
night the great   the dark   ache of tree   or rock   or
sleep   a spring in me   seep, it seep   it sleep in
me   it is a gift that I now carry   hatched in the
thistle   where   hatched in the thistle, there
I sayeth & the sky   do mumble my answer, the
wind—   away

where it goes   when it goes   in April goes it full
and fill me up on green the southern sun so hard it
hits the leaves my skin   the rushing creek the sky a
beating down   each leaf darkening to an even
darker shine & darker greenness I sayeth & I hold it
can I hold it   can I keep it   it grows it flows
through me but it flows out of me   and I let it go

throat of my throat, caught, & loosed again it rushes
back to me. most endless creek of sky a crack in
me, now pink, now flood, now steady, steady,
hold—

pale me] barely] barely] just
hold there] steady on th' [lim]b

]inthought] tho daunt
-ed inward] ly shrug'd wut [th' sun

forgot. a pale in me [low swung]flow swung
sweet] ly be] coo [rage] coo [rupt] {dove
or divin {énd}ed leaves, me {sortof sweetly sung}

in heat less loss] most
must utter] lost—

in moss] most must own] th' sun's hill'd
rim of breaking] dawn "over"] & spill't
{it piles *up*} {it fills it} (up) & {it *descends*}

from muscle, primrose, pry
first leaf then eyelid then hum
on rhyme then halt

here hear our
here held or

as mtns climb—
as mtns fall—

this soft
tantrum of the earth.

the whippoorwill— of easement
sorrows flask— of sorrow

the doe does swallow   illiterate of 'morn
come buckling down   unbuckled morn

in th' tulip breath   in th' roiling dusk
in th hazard where   th thing becomes

eye heart let eye sore no ringing
I gone down gone low in th ringing
soar in the ringing

it is in me still

shake loose the
sudden sun come
down a
ringing
thing
in
me

might grow a
season there

] wher covet
thine eyed stars
fingering th rarefied
genitals of th earth
there, I go.

there I mirrow n ounce the drunk
peony off   ] stoke
from whim must stroke
an ounce only, eye

th tangle makes
great th pearl—

eye th tangle
makes great the pearl.

overt hymn | 2 pear, pear blossom | 's fault
strok't rim from reason, up | tip 2 shaft 2 bulb, root | cup
a pain in me | thus thickly | dude I say
dude grows a root in me

as reason grows | its thorn.

held | buckling down | his antler soft
up by scuffle | muffle, muzzle | it
bit & shock't | of morning

listen— sharp th shaft |
of light does press | th sunlight caught
th birds that sing fall silent

hard   of breath | not luminous but
| ask | just press
my hand w peals
of it & lift

& lift— & lift—

dude but u know] th pear blossoms early] th flood by wut tense
muscle comes] peony in thunder] hoofs] verily I don't give a fuck
the greatness rages all around—

dude about the thing it is just a thing.
about this tip of asphodel n violet.
about this whim of rhyme about
the storm the form why
is it and then why
unwield it so

so about the lilies and
about the storms and
about the ways ones eyes do
bloom so I
curse the mud the
dew the bark of the
wet trees dripping
and the bark
of the trees
drying in sunlight
one side silver &
shining, one side
dark
& shining
& I curse the petals
in tight bundles
and the petals
falling open
full of the
yearning
for bees
but don't
make me

no owl only
no owl just
no feather no soft stroke
of air silent no
beaten breath no
nest made each
year just claw no
tooth okay a little
tooth no root okay
a little root a little
tooth small thorn
a rose a glimpse
a shock it deepens
us it calls us up
across the holler
w their wings
they beat
the air I beat
the earth.

if I cld dowse
douse if I cld this
sparse trick
-le moon [my]
burnish off then
come this grass
th rain is fine I
rein I in & eye, I
plumb

each peach for each
blossom fallen this
spring.

        that which the finch   I pry   it deep throat th
                shaft : sunlight : wingstroke
        there where | skin   wherein th muscles lie
whazzit on th rim of | de-light |
        that which eye   {the grief : the teeth}
        bend, neck {tho I : do see}
{stunned of th pink light, &, for a moment— shy}
        that which the flinch | I pray | stroke

that which | flinch
I pray, stroke.

it fill up my
mtn it shun
my ardor it
sayeth & echo
it rhyme lichen
w moss
it cross
th threshold
into language
& recedes
into verb

echo where ebb
solve for x in th valleys long
shadow, fox-light, where echo
where, echo, where shine—

ebb go where, there, wood-violet
gone utterer got uglier, as grieving is
{moth} {orion} {up} I {carry} "inside"
th blue of th creek, th blue of th sky

echo where did I leave it {today}
make mark {bruise it} & then {today}
I have left it {somewhere} where
there seems to be a lake, there

peel off, pearls of, unthunder {rain|somesun}
has the acre, catastroph, th trash, it just
piles up {srysly} & th spring-loaded
dawn done sprung done gone

where "2 slip" {mightily} {th wind}
where the bare branches raise {up} their
shook limbs, in crowning the rim, caught
in lichenlight a moment, hold it, no
echo, where

has the hollow descended {yet} the stars
has the sap hardened its buds up in me has
it come to pass {yet} the shine shined off
the creek has carried it has carried it away

"to tend what wants keeping
to fallow what wont grow"

Winter

---

not eden, Built— not by rhyme
Ringed about— moss of my
own

how the burst has sapped
my strength from me the sky, Grief, my—

all th bloom forged in the language of winter
th gullet, sleep, in me— Caress []

hollow how th egret | stands—
stutter of egret, relinquish of egret
where pray []

the last of th light each [] drop //   a limit
    [is] [drawn] around all [th] things—

th season which
has come and gone
the bitter root
in me

brief gun of morning
long gun of mourning
sip drink swallow hard hold
low only morning this
disc a lense of light
below th cloud is
bright like

up 2 prayer, there, where
each dead thing, gnarled, seems
2 breathe—

here, where
each living thing bends 2 pray

is root, in me.

and after that, when I have pickled the rose-root of my eyes
& gone nerve-numb in th blue opacity of th rushing
my tongue silver & dripping, my eyes hanging open
& gasping for breath, grasping at th shapes of things
in th grainy light—

and after that, when I have absconded w my own brightness
& felt th mud slick between my toes, & given up th dim light
that I had clung to, veritably ceded it, yes, laid it down at the
stone feet of th tall oaks silver & dripping, when I have cradled
my own face in my own face, in the nether dark & can no longer
see—

what you can speak of as varieties of sorrow

varietals//////////clementines of sorrow///// th ocean
/////wineglasses of sorrow//////hold [] my heart/////
///orchard that breaks against the tide/////my rock///
tongue bright [] my onion

                                    when I can walk one acre
                                              of sorrow
                                        through sorrow
                                          sorrows gift
                                      to walk one acre
                                    without stumbling
                              when I can call forth myself
                             from the shallows of my self
                                to be in the acre of sorrow
                             as a man is, in the tall grass
                                              of sorrow
                                in the shallows of my heart

& when I can walk through th cold blue, this blue, blue of depth,
milky blue, luminous, gulp of cold, wind, th wind that whips th
words out [of] [th space of] [yr] [my] mouth, tendril, tendril, th
breathing-out [of] [warm] breath [into th folds of th world] hills
you say, hills they are, blue on blue, hills obscuring th horizon,
hills holding th light as haze in their crevasse, mine eyes grasp
[grasp], the trembling mixture of th air

— u can see so far when the trees are leaf-less
[] like this [] in the light

[two hawks, circling—in th light suspended—
in th holler   between th hills—]

(th sharp edges of the dark limbs, th
particular sensation of each season,

th wonder of being an organism that seeks its
needs

[] that stands alone in the acre of its heart)

iris— acre— crocus— come—
absolve[d] of this—

dim [heresy]— th raw
[unbeckoned]
elation in th air

swallow me—

egret of th long neck
of th beady little eye
my heart stands on one leg
in th marshes of my heart
reflecting th silver sky
of my heart gone
numb in th cold blue water
of spring

(eagle
of my own)

th unspoken vow from dusk 2 dusk [wher th light
goes | here, this — malevolent animal
in th asters of my night, come, [] [] home—

give me back where dusk has tempered me
tempt this [my] dusk w [this] [my] darker rein
reel me from petal 2 ask, then
to gift of th sudden storm

spring peepers in th pond
that till tonight do thicken their
incessant "chorus" christ
they are loud

of all th feelings of excruciating joy— in th limp netherregions
of grief— where th coyotes yip out their glee on th cold nights
frost where th angels in excess forget themselves again, again, my
love in greener pastures, my love in dark marshes, again, my
love grown down to a darker green, th season, th endless proces-
sion, from green to darker green, at th dumb flood morning, at
th indecipherable dawn, at th steep rush— th gulleys carved each
spring— this bell in me— from blue to a darker blue, where I
have laid down, Grief— neither more nor less, th air full of its
own light, th coyotes crazy on th hills, they sound insane— how
th heart could almost burst, to drink from th spring of itself, so
cold, so blue in me, a gasp of dizzying air, I breathe it in, I grown
bright, I breathe out—

[one] needs a drink in th throat of its rushing
[one] needs a cipher of gin-bright dew
[one] needs a deep sharp pain struck hard & clear
some fine grit 2 put a polish on—

mine eyes mine eyes th rougher gaze
2 put a polish on.

this deep low groan triumph—
drink dusk till scour, this.

[having sandpapered my soul w gin I take
it up to a finer polish
on this fine particulate dusk—

it was no Orchard | in th dominion of my night | wearily &
with much strange sensation | as waves that crest & break &
gather up into themselves again— th tide | my eyes | this night
harvesting | biochemistral emblem of being-in, of being-of | of
being-for & coming-forth & becoming-only & becoming | each
organism orients itself in relation 2 desire | retreats
from pain— every
living organism seeks
its needs

[| this neuronal field atremble— what a dumb
sensory apparatus   this orchard is]

Dearth: from my perch, drunk—
th dew that dawned, done gone,
    — th memory of th storm
held on—

gone lilac for a fuse I do
gone cusp & dominion over
I do—

gone flush w a certain metabolism of light
"th multilayered substrate of th
feeling of pain"—

I do— among what wreck have I
bliss— this— dumb communion

breathe, cumulonimbus, coward
of softness—plunge, come, slowly,
into th excess— by which—
each stroke struck forth

to keep inside oneself th boundaries of one's self—
— but th wild boundlessness is a ringing thing in you
while you try to hold | th fuck still | in th stillness

— you hold
as it becomes —

[where th ache was planted, there it has spread—
where th echo answered, there it was spared—
where th bark was scored, there it has leaked sap—
what accounts for these sensations.[

how vision culls th eyes at dusk my heart
rolling [in] [th] [gentle] pornography of dusk
disintegrating [into] [th] [thick] lashes of night,
where th echo breaks down, there, where
th dim bell of my heart grows dim,
moth-like, molting in th excess
of self, how th gown grows soft
with the steady— o steady— th lashes of night

dumb, thick w sound, this rushing.

whole clenched earth this bolt
whole fist messed up this grey sky
grown greedy here this last
November.

each acre
spent— all peril each
stroke must ache for
this grim allowance of light
— moon I said, orcharding
there— u archipelago—
u mote— groan—

all low joys hum heroic
all eagles preen like finches
u iterate th story of yrself
to yrself, u preen
from self to self— prune,
copulate, amble, onward—
from self to self, go
to the utmost
horizon
touch its neck
at its utmost
horizon, th
peak of that, o
my
little
finch
taloning
my
dawn
what
joy
is
this

would have fallen
at such a slight touch
th finch, th trout lily,
th ridge of spine, heat
of skin, spineridge of earth,
each moss covered rock which
would have faltered,
deep w their own bells
where mine was ringing
as I fell

[when I have come
to th lip of dawn
I will sink
my hands in th dawn
and I will hold it there;
th muscles in my arms taut
but trembling—

earth my yield curse
whole flock thine eyes
"askance" go drowsing
split lip some sun one tree
each bloom, leaf or burst
no sexless pastoral lol each
plum | teeth each must

where I have fallen
into a deep well ringing in me—

th colors must ripen before th fall
th angels must tremble before th fold
th eagles must temper their wings
on th warm air rising up
th valley must hold sunlight
like a cup, each preening thing
profess its love at dusk, sink
down to a lower, deeper dusk

has gone, up
has orion, might
has un-decided, & again,
night—
have made me
down a
nice bed, but I,
who have felt th impatiens
rise 2 meet th poured water,
th cattail stalks raise themselves
up upright after a long hot day
th red steel hit between th spring steel
of th anvil-face & th swung steel
of th hammer I swing down,
a soreness in me,
it is ringing—
has cleft a silver ring thru me, found,
by chance, in th deep blue waters & I
Orion, swung along, this rim, this rock,
th starry field, just,
so far—

give grief its
endless pasture

I do not accept
this bell in me

o sorrows gift
is pleasure

fold me under
those hands of snow

my fever

subside the ache
n echo, blue cloth
over my eyes, th blue
of sky blue
of my river give
me just

grief— give me— just—

"one firm place"
"on which 2 stand—"

oh and absolutism. mild, darker weather,
nothing worth looking for, where is my Rilke,
my gown? my discomfort of form—

aghast, I say, lilaceous, unmingled
& particulate, this which needs us,
receive us,

like kings bitches we are—

THERE {THERE}

—one small prayer—

[I] grasp at a smaller dominion   [I] ask
that th angels b ready   having become a fracture of myself
in th Deep Blue Good Riddance of th World Amen

A Night of Dark Trees

"*our bodies have formed themselves in delicate reciprocity with th manifold textures, sounds, and shapes of th animate earth—*"
—TH SPELL OF TH SENSUOUS, DAVID ABRAM

"*only th apple can deliver th apple tree from its springtime*"
—JEAN GROSJEAN

"*Nature is a language can't you read*"

POLLINATE; BY HAND

---

polinate .by hand /dysph
or [aria{ "of th state of th flesh" what
is this [my nest] go down,
Calliope, catastrophe, my eros
from whim 2 prayer [each
wing bare | o sun o this
weird communion—]
{} several aphorisms: "th throats
of stallions th throats
of egrets th throats
of men."—2 get a grip
on [[oneself, like that—
[show me] own hive
aswarm in sunlight, own hive,
my hand, palm up [o sting]
so soft what's this
new thing in me | in this
dizzying carousel of
dew n dawn n sunday
afternoon () which kind
of coward are you, which
am I—

harnessed 2 th hollow of th sun,
drag it—

sisyphus of sun
harness of pure
light touch
my thigh
again

I wld ride
th circlet
of dew if
dawn wouldn't
so fast
expose
me—

each dim elation subsides
each bulb tries again
in spring

when I have pressed my lips
2 th wet bark, I swear, am I
going crazy

th horizon which holds me
down, is that which I
gallop along

th roaring hills where th dew comes from.
th sub-plum under th plum. th given moment
& th taken-form. even each unspoken desire,
once spoken, grows quiet in th deep breast of night.
on which winds, what tumult, which vault,
on what skeins of th bodily possible one might ride. where
th joy drained out, what shores, what rocks, what surging, this—

wine drunk my fireflies this
night [["there were elk tracks
all around th top of that mountain,
giant hooves, and a long muddy trail,
I wanted 2 follow them but
it was getting dark"

wine drunk my fireflies, in me.

th fireflies
are sparse in th dark trees—
& I, I have forced
a new cataclysm
into the darker dark

what doesn't bear plums, are cedars
what doesn't grow flowers, are rocks
th columbines cling to th rock-face
where th water seeps down & drips.
you can't restrain a river with a simple
harness, even th sturdy nets cast out let
th bright water rush through, come up
dripping. all fish are bass. th waters
abound with them.

into th raw forest, held, as if to stave
off, th surging of th forests, dogwood
studded, restrain me, you can graze yr
eyes on mine, ok, can you, in th throes
of, throw me, can you, in th ringing
non-sense, raw chord, data abuzz,
dumped out & scattered as th light
scatters in th heart, th heat, where we
are held there in stillness, we blink in
stillness, blink once for yes, close yr
eyes against th falling, dusk, I blink
once into th darkness, & hold my
breath—

THIS SUNNY DAY TH CREEK of my heart glinting this
hung crown bore down each bud or thorn in me
do you hive then, do you swallow throve & orchid
then, do you take me for a fool. we are always
already in a world of meaning, new constellations, th
peril of th day contained inside us, like a cliff
edge so high up, that if you were to look over it it would be
an endless plummeting, plummeting gaze— th angels
of my heart, hungover, saying "mercy, mercy"— in which
Virgil is insistent that the violence of man ruins
th very fabric of nature, in which Nietzsche forgets that, neither
ghost nor plant, our bodies are always & foremost creatural,
in which Elaine says "what a fucking liar. I hate him I hate
cowards."— In which I say what is this quartet struck up in me,
I did not ask for it & Dallin says "all bodies respond to spring".
Damasio says th sense of self arises from th act of knowing,
objects perceived imply a perceiver. but what if what's in you
has come unbound, & the green, & th rushing go bounding off
inside you, in search of stranger pastures.

WHO CALLS UP, AS THE SAP IS CALLED UP, when th days get hot but th nights are still cool, and th chorus of birds starts before th dawn, something is called to rise from th murky half light of your own self, a thought— no, not a thought, more like th rough outline of an unbidden desire, that, once recognized, can't be dissolved back into th rippling data in th substratum of yr body, no matter how hard you try, th grape vine once cut will steadily drip a mineral rich, slightly sweet water, exuberant, onto th ground, like this, yr desire, untethered or unbound, becomes boundless, reaching into all th wide corridors of th boundlessness of night.

OF TH UGLIEST flowers I say this: it's a shit world my petunia stuck in an obscene gesture of delight. you get to keep what is inside of you, in some sense, if you can hold it here before it changes into something else, though at some point we all have to reconcile with the real; the angels | at their nest   polyhedrons that do or do not exist— being an organism with needs & desires & th capacity for excruciating pain. I call the flowers ugly but it is something in my heart— "this, after all, is why we do most of what we do, to control what our senses will encounter." — 2 become particulate: 2 go from "shuttup bird" to "shut up yellow-throated warbler" — take me home night hawk in th high hard dusk particulate. in the lilac of my eyes. where I have placed a cold hard stone. how 2 transcend all the things is a question of th real. how 2 hold the ringing inside you a question of springtime. how to impel the sensory organism of yr body toward an imagined joy is a question that hovers between biochemistry & th void. j/k. it is a question of desire, and nailing a certain trajectory. is it the need of the bark that calls up the sap. do the blades of grass quivering in cold darkness elicit dew. I think the world evolved organisms to feel it. to crawl across its surface impelled or repelled by the feeling of it. to hold it inside of them. which we do.

MOST VINES TREMBLE. most thistles
grow thorny in th eyes— world [my]
thirst | diadem crept me heart throated region,
mist-less, mossy, kiss each leaf bud tip cuz why not
go eagle out {dendrite & gasp tho} | cut a lasso
for to hold me, gentle, gentle, down [o,
this constellation has no name— what heroic
melody will make th warm winds
bear down, & the sweet sap flow—

I, TIRESIAS, ROYALLY

I, Tiresias, royally
Fucked, on this th horizon
of my voyage, th stallions
of dawn already rearing, as if
they hear th distant bugling, as if
something in them is rearing up
inside them, only I
can hear it, already something rearing up
inside me, called to the distant bugling
as th rosy red fingers of Dawn encircle th hills—
I, Tiresias, with beating
blood, flushed w th stallions sweat,
Dawn's rosy-red fingers encircling
my neck taut at th bridle, th hawk
whose powerful soft wingstrokes
stroke th peaceful air, from where we watch it
on this big rock overlooking th valley, I,
Tiresias, overlooking th valley of my journey
& feeling the heavy thick wingbeats
in my chest, am not afraid.

it beseech th verb "to be" it become th noun "to eat"// it heaven
hath it only, only, thus [&I my self, & this, & "first"]—

u   cage   it   in
yr mouth, is it [th truth?]   Go on (with) this // my only (eye)
(bright)(not like)(the sun)   I say: "we 2 are like lighthouses"
"across th dark expanse" "we are call-notes in th coming forth"
"there is a comingling of th seasons"   "as we too comingle into
our new selves"   "I who have held"   only, only, come, at th
whim, th mercy ov—   2 trespass Wholeheartedly, in this strange
tempest(ous)(ness) of Spring—

:eyes [plunged in] forsythia, self [caught in?] forsythia—   I am
a little [] drunk | off this [relation]   this insistence |
which is Being

royally fucked me | forth—   [a hangover is a state of Grace]

& who will be my Virgil— my snow?   //   now it is th ringing,
now th tether, now th grasp—   now it is th living thing, th shook
thing, th happenstance of sky of which th lake a mirror & I, I
have bottomed out relentless in th empty field—   which is not
empty—   because I am here,   caught between th mating calls of
geese astride th world   & th light-mirror of th lake   & th lake-
mirror of th sky. there is a gasp that holds itself erect but what do you do
with it, hold it   as if some wildly fluctuating sun in you
could be contained | you seek where th old stalks are, and find the
new green—

"th true method of knowledge is experiment"
—BLAKE

I'm trying to find a workable paradigm among all th fields of
thought & desire. Honeysuckle (*Lonicera sp.*)— it hybridizes,
here. Trepid-ation of th 1st meadow, sprung be to for me, my form
th same, hwy 264, across from th rock quarry, o th truth is is it de-
scends to its own damp greenness, th sandstone shaped over Ever,
going down, I drop a rock, watch it fall— here where quartz is,
here & there strewn, th fields a tangle, to seek where th soft grass
is. to plumb th depths. poppy-bud such a light green, ooze of
whitish droplets pearling on th surface, where it was scored, with
sureness & also trepidation— profuse— even th rocks grow moss
here. in summer you can't stop th bloom, th incessant buzzing.
O arkansas— I profess— to have some real strength
in th heart—where 'th sun
don't shine' o go down deep
into th ringing field, & find th right call-note—
  I've always thought a hummingbird, o nectar
    is not so sweet— o th terror is not
      so bad, as all that, "disastrous"— I need
        a new thought, lay me
          down, in a new field
            atremble, but, in truth
              familiar... th passionflower
                vines come up only after th
                  honeysuckle, black
                    locust blooms, etc— even
                      though summer's late this year.
                        it's not that I want to find a field
                          in which things happen
                            out of order, or even
                              in which there are new things. I love

these things, th colors of them,
their chemical compositions, how I choose what
to water & what to let just, like, *go*—. it's enough to be curious,
th internet says, about what happens next. I'm resisting
a metaphor abt th path a small rock might take
into th deeper green, th plummet of it, th
way its falling is constrained by th shapes
of th vessel formed over Ever.
I am trying to find a new paradigm
among all th fields of thought
& desire, & also trying to plow
th damn meadow over, & under,
& from th side until
th quartz, th vines,
th clear water
come up w a new
hue & leak
their sap
into this
flask,
my palm

"*I did not repent of th work of my hands*"
—Psalms

"*& even th moonlight is blinding*"
—Townes

I, Tiresias, tied
to someone else's rock this vault
'ed starry heaven not
mine, & what
is this bird—

haze on th periphery   heat-lighting over Oklahoma
I recognize th bird by its wingbands, flight pattern, time of
night—   name I already call you in secret   night hawk,
dividing th sky from th sky— to speak only consonants, knowing
th vowels 2 come.   yesterday, stroking th surface, just below
th surface, of th water milky & luminous, until ripples
disintegrate the surface into a scattering of light— gets in my
eyes, dazzles me—   desire is a state of grace.   where I have
walked   to th highest peak   which is not so high   I sit
down.   a haze like this   like this   gathering in my one
good eye   denied th bloom, th vine shoots tendrils, twining
around some wire I set as a trellis   you can't stop th spring
from turning into summer.   likewise, one observes what is taking
shape inside them like watching a storm build on th radar,
watching it gather its heat and density, move east, its rolling
thunder & roving center, th pressure in th air.   I go to cover my
poppies, get my
gun.

my nymph got stuck, struck
th curr, th purr th stroke
of luck drawn back, how veined
th lightning strike me slow
o Echo follow him, which one
was turned into a tree, & which one
was ripped apart by dogs.

roe deer, python, cygnet, dove,
swallow, wallow, spear or sword
in myth he can be cruel, arrows
are for fools, we can hunt
th wild hogs, at dusk, beside my creek.
we can speak by using words
in place of other words,
or we can speak with words themselves,
or we can sleep.

& all th bodied creatures go roving

I send out a tendril, & then another one—

I'll let myself be fooled
by th killdeer, come back here
little bird, let me fix
that wing

Una Salus Victus Nullam Sperare Salutem

"th gods take th bulls hide and ejaculate on it and bury it"
—ON CONCEIVING ORION

"th arrow of this constellation points toward th star Antares, th "heart of
th scorpion" & stands poised [...] to avenge Scorpius's slaying of Orion"

O, u @ Delphi, & u
who hold th thistle, tho it
stings & u who cut
his head off, Singing,
u who forsake
th wheat for garnet
yr teeth bright
in th darkness o u
who restrain
th Dawn. th endless
crossing of th 1st
threshold, carapace,
from face, to face, shoulders
my teeth have grazed
narrow sky thunder my
dominion, night, o &
arrows, poised, try
me, u @ Pergamum,
th harbour at Troy
is grass now, "across
th fruited plain" meadow
lark, spur, man turned
into a horse to escape
his jealous wife, I'll teach you
to handle th bit, I'll give you
my grapes, tart, a little
bitter, wait—

NOTHING MAKES SENSE ABOUT THIS FLOWER

"because it would mean they have forgiven us"
—OPPEN

desire's steep rush, pasture
of atonement, cherries grown from seed—
"the kingdom of heaven" is not so great. The Dawn
is not so great. Behind th dawn there is another, bigger dawn.
When I have gone rapturous, before th fold,
when I have gone and gotten myself
fucked w th world, th worded-ness of th world,
leaf-green, pheremonal, probably drunk, crawling with
such sensations, when I have gone and tended
what wants tending, hellebore, hollyhock, angel of mercy,
don't flinch. When gods hold each other down— with
a gentle yet terrible force— yes, o make of this
th waterfall, th "glory" of th "godhead"—
thy rod and thy staff, just kidding, they
comfort me, We are already late for th threshing
"for th harvest of earth is ripe"— I do not know
how still th waters will be, where we are going, or
how green th pastures, it is already already summer, kneel down.
There is wretchedness upon th earth and many goldfinches
there is something caught in th air, here, where we are becoming
reciprocal animals, look— I hold in my hand two
cherries, and don't know how to ask
permission.

GAVE A BANQUET
UNTO TH SORROW OF IT

"In so far as my hand knows hardness or softness, and my gaze knows th moon's light....[].... certain ways th outside has of invading us and certain ways we have of meeting this invasion"
—MERLAU-PONTY

"[th bifurcation of th sensory organs].... indicates that this body is a form destined to th world [...] a sort of open circuit that completes itself only in things, in others, in th encompassing earth"

Idolatry of th verge. crest of an echo, solipsism
of th void, sweet root-flesh of th root. Hassle of sun,
communion of jupiter, liturgy of geese & lakes.
th river of silence as of a river of light where you were
late to your own baptism, naked, by th highway, a million
miles from th center of th earth. Paradigm of objects in motion,
declension of th verb "to be"— dripping, "come unto me"—arch-
angel— of th lonesome earth, th vultures raising off th body in
slow motion— th heat from th engine still hot under me. I can-
not singlehandedly baptize th whole wilderness. I will start
with this river.

and who will prepare th way before me, son of
man, glistening in th green waters. we are in-
extricable from th dna of th world around us, our senses
comingled with th sensed "without which there would be no
possibility of experience" listen, I'm trying to tell you something,
even though I can't hear myself above th ringing darkness,
th stars, mastiffs and echos, count me among yr numberless
eons of seed, acres of permission, parallax of clover, axle of
rhyme upon skin, orbit of pure need. mars is cresting th
southeastern horizon, like a little bitch chasing his shadow
love is not a harbour, there is no such thing as a gift.

th magnolias are still blooming in Ozark,
th dam, th river, th vision of it; seethe. "damn near
put a hurt on me" [*in me— in me— in me—*]
thick w foam— riddled w gesture
opiate of form— th body— stunning— "had a good
spawn there" "I've fished
with minnows smaller
than these" | th Lawlessness of Arkansas
[lawlessness is a state of Grace] where my heart
stands like a lonely bird, fishing from th dark rocks— Unclench
th great dam o Arkansas of my soul, untriumphant
this night.   line of white
egrets along th writhing edge where th
water rears up. was it fear
that kept you— how did you know
how to hold back th flood?

LET TH DISASTER BEGIN

— why

is it so soft who
knew what

bloom ache
must force —

WHAT THY FUCK

"what is it that will last"
—TENNYSON

to trespass— on eyelid and armpit
alike— summers lake of summer— all
th lakes of summer— take me
by my horns, my argonaut— o captain—pollen
on th lake— wait— it is not a good day
for th baptism— I wanted 2 get fucked
in all th most beautiful places of summer—
not this— how far down does it go— what
cool dark gathers in th tangled forest, what
deep dark stares back at yr face— what is it
right in front of you, in a flash of lightning, then
we wait for the thunder, then
the thunder comes— something
just under th surface— gather
"thine wits"— "it usually takes
stronger signals of distress
to elicit an appropriate response"
what is it that you are trying to show me,
in that handful of dust — those are not
my horns—what is it
that is pawing at yr lip—

Th Ecstasy of St Theresa, or
How strange 2 b in a continous state of transcendence

---

*"beside her, a smiling seraph delicately uncovers Theresa's breast to ease
th path of his arrow."*

"if that's a look of divine ecstasy, I know all about it"

toes of grace and
knees of grace and
mercy of th stubborn
grace of th tangled
heart of grace mime
me mimicry of mourning
doves
of grace of th night storm
where we are baptized
in th thunder and th
flashes
of lightning
of grace, bower—
"I will make my love a—"
what is a sepulcher rough
neck of grace chapel
in th woods th bent ribs
of rafters where grace
trembles before this thistle
mercy wound fig of grace, o
2 b grateful: be grateful, graceless
animal of th bent
stalks, eyes and eyelids and
lips of grace teeth of
grace how 2 learn
what is necessary
of grace, what is asked of u,

by grace, and will u kneel before it,
in th deep
woods long spine
aching river flowing
into th lake
of grace, plunge
of th taut
muscle soft
into grace
I come.

take one form and fill th vessel
take one form and chase th echo
take one from among th many
grasp it by its mollusc
take one stroke and then hold back
th next
take one animate thing and breathe on it
take one instance and replicate it
hold yr face right up 2 my face night sky
stuck in a constellation
of imprecise grace, take one given thing
and give it back
take one fig leaf and place it over
take one flower and then another

while th daffodil is in th field there can b no clover
when rigid is th paradigm— bend over—
bathe me in th glory
creature fireflies
of my mouth in th dark
land of night where I stood
wrecked, un-angel'd
barefoot beside the lake—
I feel my neck move
under my own hand.

make it b my heart
ringing like a lonely field
I am of th echo, crave
th fold—

teeth where u have
eyes where u have
hands where u feel
th soft arch of feet th
arc of breath between
lips of breath th lips
of night comes down
th shaft—so soft—so
common this day is each
day as unbidden as
th next—

I am in th unbidden
desire of
grace's endless
endless night

"But as a matter of fact, the modern anachronism is not the union
of body and soul [...]but its demure separation into sensual and
spiritual experience."

"within th basilica"

"is held aloft on th fingertips"

"he had betrayed th integrity of stone"

"it is this precise moment, both spiritual and carnal, that Bernini
tries to seize"

oh my speckled
speckled egg of summers
mists and dawns
unquenching firmament of boughs
thrown at th doorways and th afterthoughts
and aftershocks of morning, there
where I have cleft a single note
gone arcing, left to its own
devices as th weeds
unfurl, grow unruly
there th tempest reigns
and carves its
high throne mighty
is th sword make of
me th sword th tempest
shake from these boughs
loose th summer petals
th full undisclosure
of my own—

o go now
fool where I have given u
unto th silence, let it
break you
truck tire + mirror
ounce of summer,
you have already
let it pass, this thing
a million fish
in yr empty hands
don't pass me th god
forsaken boughs, I like mine
full of th early
cherry blossoms I will
take th evening light,
th waning moon, against

all rational consideration, against
th grainy fields of night, this is my
constellation, shape of many
many forms
reconfiguring itself
in th empty
empty field of night—
why don't you ever
come to me—I have made this
bower, I have picked
each red flower
and put it in a vase, I have said
mercy is upon th eyes
of all th gods and I,
I will kneel
at their feet they that
anointeth me, I that
annointeth them, each
to each, w their teeth, their
eyelids, their silence
unto th shape of things
to come I go
like a little fish
while th great
river
writhes milky and
luminous around me, say again
those things, freaked animal
of th verge, hymnal
by which all known things
proceed in th countless
terrors of our own
dusk, our own
annunciation

AS MUCH A WOLF AS A SHEPHERD,
OR A CURSE

"what does your body proclaim of your soul"
—NIETZSCHE

"swear to me, with one hand on th bountiful earth
and th other hand on th glistening sea"
—ILIAD

I.

the sun is my shepherd and I am a wolf
to ease th aching blood from me

walk until you hear th sound of water
over rocks— I'd marry you in stillness,
in quietness— and stillness— in secret,
Achilles, death of my death, dream
of a thousand sons, yr ankle, curved
arch of yr foot, yr bronze helmet
with its frightening plume.

my mother, and a weapon
my mother, and a ship.

where the fault lies, there th earth shudders,
where the horizon is a thin line forever tipping over
where the peaches fall, it is summer,
ravens are west of the rockies, here it is only crows.

{from me— from me— from me—}

where is the kingdom of heaven
where is the rocky mount

it is a kind of hymn.
it has been a kind of hymn.
one could consider it a hymnal.
I like a freshly polished lake.
did you change your mind, o
deeply weird birds of my soul,
where my angels aren't. O echo,
wingbeat, chain on chain on wet rock—
the kingfishers are fighting upriver
something has gotten lost,
something that was important—

I will call down each leaf
but nothing will tremble,
nothing will fall

death, call it death—
the death of a loved one, that you will love
forever. call it death, th wide embrace of sky,
north star cold of my heart, yr arms outstretched
from scorpio to opposite horizon, no,
north is a little further, wider on. can you hold this
whole half of sky, no, it is too big, call it
a small death, or a big one. call it grief
that holds you in those wide, strong arms.

II.

where is it that th sweet breath
comes as mist from these very rocks,
which place can I touch—

no place will remain untouched
and you will never rest, at last.

dove-killer

in th high-gone light

leash is th rim by which

inaction vrs action vrs consequence

what never was has never been

rhymes abscond w their Own

Orion

other words for mercy

is molting even a thing anymore

these are embers that were green
wood

when th meadow has withheld permission

the word "lure" on th tongue

where my sorrow has answered itself
with a weirder sorrow

the river fed by th heavens

which was th saint in th wilderness
but not yet dismay

touch is th mechanism by which

everything you love | is in the world

"salvation"

just because you washed
your feet with snow...

unlash him,
he can drown—

none of us have a god
at our backs to hold up
the dawn for us, like you, Odysseus, and so I go,
to th river without you, enduring
th interweaving of my own
patience & impatience, distilling
something heavy from th heavy air, drink
warm beer on th hood of my truck
& watch th blue dark sky change,
reflected in th surface of th water
between th dark line of trees
dense w tiny flashes of light
& th river & th sky
like two corridors that meet
between them, never touching,
both sinking down & down
to a deeper,
darker dark.

GENTLY INTO TH WIND, BOYS——, OR
IT IS MUDDY, THERE'S NO TRUTH TO IT——

"how best to orient oneself in th surrounding terrain"

"how far is th sunset? we shld go faster——"

it was when th chickweed was blue
along th edges— shore— road—

it was when th berries were ripening
even in th shade

it was in th long gestation of th meadow
and th still surface of th lake

it was in th time when kneeling down meant nothing
even unto th sign of itself, th time between
Imaginary and Becoming, when th air hangs still,
it was in th time where blood was easily
turned to water, or to beer, and back to blood
and certain eyes needed guarding—
it was in th high hot season of summer
when we arrived— everything
was merciless— even th stars
grew too bright
and felt like curses

where need has placed its seed of desire
but where was th wind— where
were th horses—

diagram of all possibilities;
altair, deneb, vega
fuck me right up w this
my heart is made out of seeds
trampled by th endless
hooves of night

    I sleep in th field next to my truck, trying to remember
    something important—

this earth
I call my home. for th days of light
are upon us. for th days
of light are also days of reckoning—

prey animals just freeze in place, this tells us
something about th dangers of motion.

what causes you
joy will bring you suffering

when I have grieved and not done w grieving
when I have come, and not done w coming,
came to th far edge of th dark field strung w asters,
alone in th wide field of night—
when I have laid down
like a lonely dog, drunk
& restless, awake beside
th dawn (beside myself at dawn)

when I have claimed a shape of stars—
bitches can you please let off me, soon.

when I have watched th moon go down
and known no sin
so great

as that which one sins against ones own body
in th empty field of night, w mars so close and

"every angel is terrifying"

to saturn I sacrifice 3 boughs
of tent caterpillars ‖ beam
of light from earth & doused w gasoline:
in this way I might save my persimmon tree,
—Andromeda, Cygnus, a new chill in
th evening air—
& be a man who walks upon th earth

at th far mouth of th lake, where my
creek runs in

th sun wraps around th valley, hills
of my green heart dark w foreboding,
lit w foreboding—

green gem of place
green heart of summer
green heron on th shore
how could I not, in th heart of th lake,
how could I not—

"not 2 b scoffed at, are th radiant gifts of th gods"

"if th cooked sprout of th seed is bitter, don't eat it"

heaven makes a beak of itself, twigs, soft
down. for strength of heart bears upon th skull
& small seeds scatter in th wind

I would be as th small bird torn
apart by th hawk

these ones that were ripened in th shade
are not so sweet.

th wind in yr orchard th
swirling wind th limbs of yr orchard th
hard fruit th bitter fruit th gaze across
a green expanse whipped by such a wind
as this th pear tree hit hard
by a late frost th rough bark
th inevitable turning of th seasons th
wind in my hair how th wind
whips th breath from my mouth
each word pulled from my mouth

it forces silence upon my mouth
it teaches my skin a lesson
my shadow is th shadow of a place

I am in th punishment of th cathedral
I am deep in th punishment of th cathedral

"GIRL ON HER KNEES DISCHARGES A FLOWER BASKET"

---

begat each stone each seed hold forth
this night please let each star
be just a star please lord again

rake th whole acre of stars down
o lord have mercy on

"we all got to be baptized
whether we need it or not"

is yr wild indigo blooming
are th photoreceptors
in yr eyes ready for what happens next
have you taken over th body by force
has th chemical expanse washed over u, wrung
u out, hung u up
to dry in th sun, linen of my eyes,
blue quilt, blue washcloth, blue sky,
plunge & combat, lie— even th rocks
can stand up and answer, why
can't you.

renounce each gift one
by one each seed, each need,
give it back, its pressure
there, each word a prayer, lost
in th darker dusk, th need
lost in th graceless
form
of an animal at dusk

CYGNUS TH SWAN

what one might ask of th silence, paradigm
of th frozen verb, heart of a bird, o heavens no, lord
knows th terror there, pearls of my thoughts
go rolling, I have spilled them, I clutch & cast about—
should I turn into a long-legged bird, a reed,
or a small tree— all of my eyes,
garnets, teeth, rhyme me— you can pitch
yr fits w silence— I "though
my flower th same"— draw my bow, close
both eyes;
take aim—

I will rein my one angel back, stumble
my own self up, bull-thistle
& cardinal-flower, sworn,
by my own river, naked in all
th world, th aralias
bloom while their leaves
turn deep violet, dark
red, devil's-
walking stick,
Mercy is a verb.
Mercy, mercy, call off th dogs
it's just me, remember—

call off
th dogs, it's

just me

remember—

WHAT THAT MOUTH DO

"I make a boat out of an apple tree / both ends are golden"
—ROBIN BLASER

"A slight wound to be sure, but fatal"
—OVID, OF A MAN TURNED INTO AN EAGLE AND SHOT,
WHOSE WOUND MADE HIM UNABLE TO FLY

for courage is upon th lips [prey
for courage [leaf
for courage is [grief is
for courage is upon th grace
& th graceless, alike— th ladder
up 2 heaven; "what you do is, you
take a small saw, and"— yellow
against th blue— for courage,
oh get down from there, all
of you, spinning in th heavens
like fools, I will drop
each star into th lake, where
my heart, a gizzard, greedy and
luminous, grinds them, you know how
the water here is pearly around us—
as each mirror shuts its eye,
for courage [drop
yr gun, & go—

"samples of men, mere specimens"
—OVID

"amid th waves, we die of thirst"
—IANTHES, OVID

mercy is a verb
dire portent
is th swan, milky
cum of heavens "strewn"
stretches before th swan
& "straight on till morning"
mercy by th river
mercy in th dark trees
mercy of th imaginary
verb, need, hurt, let
loose, two hawks down
below I said mercy
is upon th shadow
and th shadow
upon th rocks, two shadows
gliding along th rocks below, in silence, I said
mercy in th relentless surface of th lake,
I whispered it into th neck
of th river where it feeds into
th lake, muscadine on th shores,
felt th warm breath leave my lips
held to th neck of th lake, felt th
waves of cooler or warmer air
across th surface of th lake, across th
surface of our skin, rolling over
the surface of our skin off th lake,

I whisper, mercy, I would like
to be forgiven by the lake, whole
summer, two shadows gliding along
th rocks below, I spit out
th bitter seeds of th muscadines
hanging low at th throat

I don't want to bathe in th cold water ｜I take
off my clothes— I bathe in th cold water, o lead me,
Ianthes, hold   me   down   by [th throat of] th river
hold me [down by] th river, blue   shirt, blue gaze of sky,
crust upon th lips and heart   crust of sky silent as any god
great   blue heron overhead   silent as th changing sky
"there's a part of me that prays"   th whole world
stretching   out from th center of yr chest   held under th dark
surface   of th dark water— fingertips, toes, lips,   hair in th dark
water   and small fish, some stars, my dog on th rocks sleeping,
headlights, hallelujah,   one cardinal flower glowing deep red
in th moonlight, I hold it in my minds eye, nothing is allowed
to coalesce, each universe suspended, spinning, separate "heaven's
just a sin away"   my neighbors are shooting guns   thru th
woods o   (baby, baby)
strike me true

I don't say daffodil when it is full on summer, just so
I expect a sort of radical honesty from my surroundings

"but neither sorrow nor tears nor fear delayed me, lifting
his body from the ground, and on these shoulders,
these shoulders, mine, I bore Achilles' body,
armor and all, arms which once more I ask
to bear: heavy they are, but I can bear them"
—ODYSSEUS' CLAIM ON ACHILLES' ARMOR, OVID

I

high above th earth]] green crust of sin— green bloom
upon th earth [[high & deep upon th earth]] dendritic watershed
of th Arkansas]] plume & vein of my green heart [[neck where th
sky arches, neck of th swan, sworn, his hands, bow loose at his side

]] shit I will not say out loud]] O daffodil
my winter— what I know—

]]weary of

]]great as th throat of sky, clenched
]]as th throat of sky

[[for th days of night are upon us
[[for th days of night are also days of reckoning

incandescent imprint of th tree on eyelid, blue sun, ore & fault,
vein, oar, pair, pare, steer, cleave, idle, clear, breathe, gently | on
my face— like that—

then crows, I am leaving {leaving} each place— a reflection held
up to th sky — of each thing— you have to trust me— simple—
to hold yr breath— in all th world.

a body is an animal— a body is a pack of crows alighting on each
tree— I am each tree—

you are not my own.

[wasp and quartz, each
which, pain— each which
/ burst—

chew tobacco, where it stings

orchid of th most bitter, bitter tongue

{or, root

II

is that salt— or is it snow— those terrestrial
crop circles spun by th endless endless combines
of my heart, dappled, striated, pierced, crisscrossed,
veined, wearily, patiently, painfully, I go.
my legs are numb and tingly, th long
barrel of my rifle hot, th cattails bruised and battered, th
sky bruised and ringing, th iris that blooms in
th winter of my eyes turns its bruised eye to th ground
scattered w buckshot. I will gag th lilies w a gasoline soaked rag,
come spring. stack tires around my fig trees in th snow. oscillat-
ing wildly between chickadee and bird of prey, between snake and
discarded skin, I roam, eagleless, un-nouned, an arch and a bridge
between myself and time, an echo and rhyme in th deep baptisms.

I want to call into question th holiness of this forest;

th snake that lives in my throat; th warm air
of th wingbeats of yr breath around my face.

III

we shoot guns until we run out of bullets
[[I will say unto you
there is no merciful
voluptuous
passerine
voluminous in th folds of night there is no
mercy upon th lips and teeth and watersheds

of Arkansas, all words go bad
into th night ringing like a dull bell
in th heart where each stroke disintegrates
around yr swollen face, eyes, where I have placed
my own self, ringing into th voluminous folds of night

and we are out of bullets and it is cold
and each word goes weirdly
into th cold silence of th night
and mercy is not a verb, I will
coppice my fig trees, I will
lay th body down.

[[I will ask you to lay th body down

IV

yr teeth | some fruit

      verily

      each

          grasp each

      | which pit

   whose hand

apostate

apophatic
| no falcon

      him that is th flute
      & th reaper of th flute
      firm fleshed fruit ripening
      in November— confusion
      of many forms—

]"some bright morning"
]beeswax on th orchids &
 beercans in th bath

negative theophanies

               by mine own eyes

                  once

       & then again

           by my own hand

V

hear me
u of th
north wind cold first
frost flower each
soft blown breath, bow
down there is only
permission in th answer,
permission in th field
permission in th marsh
and of the bitter flower,
falcons, nests,
get a grip on,
sunked fruit, got a
whitish bloom there, hardens
th sugars up under th
skin, there, each
coyote dead by th highway, u
ride it out w what grace
u can muster, listen
to me and I will tell you:
u must stand
as each flower
must stand, acrid
persimmon, stupid
hawk circling
in th still air
of yr heart go
on, get
up
]]

VI

this is not a condemnation, but neither is it a prayer.

VII

                          think of th bacchic rites
                              think of grief
                  think of summer, of every summer, think
                  of grief, think of th best sex you've ever had,
                  think of bodies in pain, think of th sensation
                     of relief, th palliative need, think of grief.
                              think of th act of laying
                     th body into th grave, think of alms, of
                  th act of honoring, receiving honor, kneeling,
                  being bound, think of memory. think of summer,
            laying th body down, remember digging, think of th
                  body you would turn to, blue shirt, a noise
            made half in th nose, half in th throat, think of
                  turning over in yr sleep, now a noise
            made mostly in th mouth and throat, think
                     of bodies sleeping, turning over
                     in their sleep, think of grief. each
                     masterpiece was made piece by piece.
                  think of th sensation of loss, think of th
                  sensation of coming, think of things to
                  hold in yr hands, think of cups, and dirt,
                  think of skin, and eyes, and teeth. bite
                          th blue cloth and think of
                     grief. think of summer. think of
                          th memory of th loss.

"that was not dew upon them"
—Ovid

made a punishing necklace—
unto th heavens— go— what th
heaviness must ask— go— then—into
oh go into— god Damn— this
persimmon of frost— this
unarchable heaviness— upon me
— god— not to breathe— heavily— th god
is snoring— this— is a disaster— they say—
and I agree— damn— that's heavy, a heaviness,
this— or awkward— this— give me back
th necklace of those things— this summer— the body—
time— sullen as my heart which was an eagle,
stood, upset, preening, in th mirror of th sky

because these are th confines of language

how everything
just— like— is, as it is becoming
what it was—

                              soot from stood, from hoof
                           here from ash, steer, horizon
                       is my name o preen, all preening things,
               for dawn does come and you, you must stand, naked
               before th window, like a fool, dick limp, as if you
                           didn't know what was happening
                       to you— in you— in this opera each culprit

lies, then begs, & then, eventually kneels— are you ready
to kneel, yet,
when you are done lying on yr belly like a snake, felt yr
heart turn and turn again— in th back
of this truck— where it was too cold— each letter of my
breath
breathed back— no angel— yr eyes, each non
angel of summer— assholes— I swear— so go
—this heaviness upon me—
{on me— in me—}
what I need is
to reach out, to reach
some real place
in all of this.

flint-shaped, heavy as a tooth,
licked, by bower, happenstance, place, has
come— each eyes, snake eyes, withheld, then gave
permission, when th frost—each fruit—th
flower was, and given, gave then

from ash—white box—snow is
— is isn't, is—there—in th snow—
half moonlight— half face— take this
fruit— how grief is— all I can say
is what it is to keep on living, be a thing
around th other things— I don't know
anything about anything about being:
we are not equipped for this.

the change had already taken place— in me—
in me— in me—] punish yrself in th stillness—
it is {will be} a gentle punish— {these} shores, low
graves, sunlight, some crows— {in me, persist—}
hold [this] in]mouth {on}]chest   [hold this] in some stillness
{give back} one stone and where we | sat down :   a stillness— go
now— and then another stone: that love
expands or contracts around us
impregnating all th things

what each place asks of us—for it had begun
swollen as th new day— even tho we don't know
what to do with it— even in th thin light—
have mercy— on each new day full
of {tendrils | angels | eyes}
— what right do I have—
to any of this—

th ozark
witch-hazel is blooming, December 2018

DO NOT BE TH NORTH WIND—
[FIG

---

everyone knows that that's a grave
|| for morning is upon th lips
and a bitter mist is upon th lips:
everyone knows that you are digging a grave

our heart [s]
how [we each] set forth in our mission

"have thy tools ready"
"upon this crystal-less shore"

where each grip lay, was wanted,
which wrung, done ringing, waned, which sun
set there, which ring held briefly, wet, set glinting
in th sun—

bitter triumph | speak, wasp
rose quartz on th shores where I have left them

when I have not known how to fill myself up
on creek or sky or strange light, when I have come
again to the same place: I wish
I could take out my eyes and clean them
I'm getting sick of this place

[[a sore and ringing purple mist
upon the ~~lips~~ eyes | everyone knows
you must lay th body ~~down~~ to rest

when I have woken in th painful moonlight
when I will lay a flower down
where I will lay
a flower, down

the change had already taken place, in me

    "sore" "which, in a way
    is very sweet"

each need abates. each baited thing
awaits. each persimmon needs th
frost, each sweet thing falls to earth

is what is feminine in me defined
by sorrow

is what is feminine in me defined
by sorrow

is what is feminine in me defined
by sorrow

palindrome] emote

[wishless ferry

[rose of Charon

[kiss my forehead
[purple, finch

[of a lazy | hungover | snow

go now, into th frost, my flower, Pearl,
my heart, abandon— for speed—
it will be months before th trout lilies come up
— there is nothing to do but wait:
everyone knows you are digging a grace

[as I lay th body down
[as we lay th body down
[as you lay th body down
in the grave I dug
in th mist upon th shore
I am getting sick of this place

th great rope which tethers earth 2 sky, bound
at th wrists and ankles, gently
but with a terrible force, Andromeda, my breath—
th condensation on th glass— reach up—
o each body, weird body— arms, legs, feet—
extant in space—
to ask | 2 b christened
by all that gathers in th cool dusk—
— to stand up— what is it that gathers
in th cool dusk
at yr face— yr hands, unbound,
open now, to let th cool air though, whole
night, each season, no rhyme, no nothing,
pitched forward, where yr lips have passed over in silence
th stillness of yr autumn th shallow waters
of th lake of yr heart full of frogs,
eels and fish and small molluscs, small rocks,
a yellow-crowned night heron stalking them
on th white riverbed, th berries
are done, th geese are going, th lake
is driven dark and mad w wind, th bluedark sky
of yr heart, when it has stopped raining
and I am in th meadow still, untethered from th sky
and all around is wind, wind, th clouds
driven across th sky in all directions
and the geese are flying south again
and every word you speak is false
and th sky like an idiot runs itself into th ground, drunk,
staggering—scattering th small hard seeds
  [[are those horns— where is th moon— I don't
know— how to help you— now—]]

before wheeling off again, seeking
its leash, its
palm & open
pasture wider,
farther on.

Holy Spirit GTFO

"sleep, shepherd, it doesn't matter where"
—Jacques Dupin

who has taken me back and forth behind the clover
who has split the soft lip of fog at dawn
who has spoken words into my mouth who has put
their tongue against the salty eyelids of morning,
curséd tongue, sweet tongue, mouth of corn-silk,
one snake, dumb tongue of morning—
cursed the genitals between the legs—holy
spirit— who has begged forgiveness
from th small birds
just now starting in the trees around—

holy spirit you are welcome here

that which was once seamless, now
has a hem—

when we felt that we were promised sun, and were given none
when we felt th salt wind blow up from th gulf— I, Virgil,
standing, as I like to do, in a place surrounded by th "whole
world"—
on this cliff— there's a fucking— ache in it my dude, it will
settle on th ache in you— I can smell it on th air, the blossoms
ache—

I know it— I'm telling you—
because I'm your friend—

put that edge on it— sharp— like th devil said.
fuck Saint and Paradise and Cardinal and Calvary

fuck Vision and Holy and Void
fuck down deep in th heart where th deep waves are fuck
everything in th sky. th magpies bend. the grackles are all eyes.
I do not forgive the wind.
a small death takes place in th heart of each tree.

holy spirit you are welcome here

& some, for me, bright star, radiant— this night
this night escapes us, more bud than fruit, single flame, most remain
each day each thing remains, where I have placed it,
the dead body of the dead snake writhing on the table
for hours, its head in a coffee can nearby

I can still feel its body moving, muscley in my grip, for hours after

if you pinch, & squeeze, you can milk the venom out
later, it rots in that jar because the lid was bad—

the rotten head of the rotten snake in the rotten
venom of its rotten night—

holy spirit you are welcome here

— whose skies is this—today—and after—when I have
to go— why is it that each day we make again
a man—who are you kissing, in that room
with all th windows— and stand in different postures, in
th constellation of ourselves— your body was of the place.

from my mount and serpent there

my ankle, my heart, my nonsense, free me
body of earth, causality and generation

still wounded, dog, get down, my knees, alloy
and circumcision and anguish, having taken
to th hot steel over the knife, gemstone and
masculinity and prayer, where my lips are,
tonight, what is the story— what is the name
of the knife?

I'm nervous about something

[th body's involuntary
th bodys involuntary—]

there might have been an ambush in it
it might have been hidden in a bush
which might, also have been burning, yes,
like this, o get out of there
no voice of god, no prayer,
just "the thing itself"—

your body was of the place—[but which was the body,
and which was the place?]—that which was once greedy
of th grace

and th graceless alike
that which was once greedy of the light—close your eyes—
o, man—if I could only find a place—

to get thrown—violently—as if from
two (2) horses—as if— disequilibrium of cities & forests,
horn and cornucopia of man—causeway and viaduct and
great bore-holes bored under the highways—whatever
love encompasses— announces— distains—

it is like as if it is a living thing
I was afraid—and—
I was afraid

along the thin edge of grace
where grace bleeds into a new and different grace
it was just the edge that I was on
it is just the edge that I am on

holy spirit— it is with a heavy heart—
that I take into my mouth—

make the grace stand in th cold of itself
trembling in th grace of itself nuthatch
on th spring bark upside-down in th cold
grace hard nipples in th kitchen little
winter berries in th feeders just enough

a motif—a motive—a pattern—premonition
dust-dust-dust-dust— we are incapable of sin

holy spirit you are welcome here

1st communion, February 17th 2019

"I don't think I could make this decision before god"

you blaspheme of desire | you "blaspheme" / "desire"
the thin line of horizon where you are

"absconded" / "in ambush"

"since we've got no place 2 place"

I was unspeakable to the language of this

holy spirit you are welcome here

MERCY
{ADDENDUM}

"he does not know th horses' names"
—OF PHAETHON, SON OF TH SUN-GOD, DRIVING TH CHARIOT OF
TH SUN & REALIZING HOW OUT OF CONTROL TH CHARIOT IS.

Other words for Mercy

is that the shadow of a hawk

on earth as it is
on earth as it is
on earth as it is
on earth as it is
on earth as it is
on earth as it is
on earth as it is
on earth as it is
on earth as it is
on earth as it is
on earth as it is
on earth as it is
on earth as it is
on earth as it is
on earth as it is
on earth as it is
on earth as it is
on earth as it is

in heaven | then beg

Other Words for Mercy

rain driven hard across th surface of th lake

OTHER WORDS FOR MERCY

I can be gentle

THE MYTH OF MALE VIRILITY

maybe it's th rain that just wont come

OTHER WORDS FOR MERCY

th chastised wolf becomes th dog

OTHER WORDS FOR MERCY

"making a sound not human, but a sound no stag could utter either"

call off th dogs it's just me remember

find one form and then let loose another

OTHER WORDS FOR MERCY

don't | stop

CODY-ROSE CLEVIDENCE is the author of *BEAST FEAST*; *Flung/ Throne*; *TWANG*; *Listen My Friend, This is the Dream I Dreamed Last Night*; and several handsome chapbooks. They live in the Arkansas Ozarks with their assorted animals named after other animals.

NIGHTBOAT BOOKS

Nightboat Books, a nonprofit organization, seeks to develop audiences for writers whose work resists convention and transcends boundaries. We publish books rich with poignancy, intelligence, and risk. Please visit nightboat.org to learn about our titles and how you can support our future publications.

The following individuals have supported the publication of this book. We thank them for their generosity and commitment to the mission of Nightboat Books:

Kazim Ali
Anonymous (4)
Abraham Avnisan
Jean C. Ballantyne
The Robert C. Brooks Revocable Trust
Amanda Greenberger
Rachel Lithgow
Anne Marie Macari
Elizabeth Madans
Elizabeth Motika
Thomas Shardlow
Benjamin Taylor
Jerrie Whitfield & Richard Motika

This book is made possible in part, by grants from the New York City Department of Cultural Affairs in partnership with the City Council and the New York State Council on the Arts Literature Program.